INTO THE DARK

Brendan Tripp

ESCHATON™
BOOKS

http://EschatonBooks.com
978-1-57353-014-9

THE SORCERER'S FLAME, TRIUMPHANT

Fire,
and bands of power come to rise.
What orbs aglow
the power of this lowland give?
Clouds spread,
soft threatening blanket,
In grey's full strata formed.
They define the upper limits
and cordon off more welcomed skies.
This zone embattled withers
and is buffeted by winds.
What wizard's call is heard here
by this nature so unnatural,
these sights of vision's bane?
Fire,
again the flash illumines
red to blue and blue to red,
hidden lips peal laughter
and the horizon seeks to end!
There shifts the land
and trees reject their rooting,
close comes the sky,
We are undone, we are undone,
the road is barren,
the staff has been consumed.

WAVE VALENCE: ONE FORM

The reflection's a-glimmer
and moves rilling through:
    limits sometimes holding shine,
    with seemly clear and pleasantry.
In these few hours
there is little self,
but some veiled absence
hanging over the world:
    the wavelengths conjoined
    in a semblance of one.
These far seldom times
come encased by the flow:
    all obstreperous habits
    silted down, washed clean.
No notions of action
come to the mind.
No impulses surface
to splash ripples across the calm.

ORGASM ... ARCHITECTURE

These temples blossom,
to cathedrals mature.
Strange fertile fields
give these generation,
dark the alternate radiation
which builds on this stone.
What expanse
such cacophonic reaching
these habitants have,
they are antithetical,
they clone the genesis flow.
Strange structures these,
strange rafts and flotsam
drifting.

LISTENING TO CAGE'S "EMPTY WORDS"

1
Sometimes that, too, comes up.
Sometime many of these
are brought.
Extraction comes of me
and I am the pool,
within and without the bearings
of habitual visage.
Inside is the jewel.
Inside is real being.
Dust hangs heavy and distracts,
heavenly angels,
excuses, believe no alibi:
>The halls are stone
>they echo and vague;
>my feet are soft and pad
>nearly silent.
I need to find an opening.
Knock.
Inner sanctum admit,
thyself admit.
Sun filtered rays this strange table lit,
too covered,
too warm, blanketed,
the gleam is there,
Where is the gleam?

2
Reason erupts
and is hallowed.
Direction drives, insistent,
purposeful but careless,
it flies the arrow,
chasing the target retreating
as all average
to form the one insistent vector,
the single true force,
the signpost of lives.
>It is red,
>it is yellow,
>the color is total,
>the heading unique.
It seeks unlidding.
It drives to open.

3
The gaming folds,
in stillness comes taut.
The catacombs are madness,
the shade of night rides high:
    It orients the stars
    in patterns of its own design.
    We can not read these runic forms,
    they are the language of the other side.
Mirrors to us
are as walls.
All are the intimation,
few are the fulfillment
to permeate only sight.
The secrets lie in safety,
the locks hold firm
and the altar is forbidden.
Parting violence
shatters,
rifts spread out
and encompass worlds in passing.
Containments are lost,
tabernacles defiled.
    To intersect;
    to be these doors.
Identifying finally,
clawing at raw light,
we scream in frustration
and curse for the sky.

WITHOUT THESE LIGHTS, FORLORN

Is there nothing left, then,
no particulate ghost
wafting cross the beams of this singular moon?
Has all been strangled,
pressed to foreign service and given new frame?

The shadows of innocence pass,
as false visions of unstable night,
they shimmer in grey junctures,
too subtly pleading for unfathomed paths
and trailing an ache in the slipstream of their dissolve.

Once was green, and light, and seasons of spring,
once was explosions of question
and the fervor of vital madness.
Are there truly no remains
to tide us through these days?

LONG WINTER COME UPON US

What now, you angels,
now that the leaves have fallen
and summer grasses turned to dust?
Are all these plains
forever given to the winter's grasp?
How long will life be buried
in deep cold tombs and longer nights,
how long this wind continue
with hostile blasts and blades of ice?
What courses are these clouds to take,
which points are you to steer?
And, are we but to wait our time
forever through these years?

BY HIEROPHANTIC STEERAGE

Hold, dancer,
these are not the steps,
your flagstone leapings have traced a fault,
these temple precincts witness.
By these robes I scan your path.
By this scepter I call your time.
In these tracings I hold the lore,
your ancestral decree.
    None of these pillars here
    are as fragile
    as the crystal from which your dance is spun.
Your weavings must hold to all the ancient dictates,
and must cycle with the sinking of the stars.
Hold, dancer,
lest your course be falsely set.

THE NIGHT OF RAVENS

So, sinister shadows,
so, shades of the night,
so, darkness
and all denizens herewith:
    we are assembled
    we are here.
Here is the dance,
here is the rite,
we are the priests
of light and of dark,
    this is the battle,
    Golgotha resurgent.
You are the void,
I am the spark,
I spawn generations,
beings resplendent,
    to fill your absence
    to unempty your dark.

These weapons dire
carpet the heavens
and darken this globe,
they seem the night of ravens
loosed upon unknowing sheep.

THE RINGS OF COLD

The steam rises and curls,
holding the crisper air,
then flees to the refuge
of infinite smallness.
This winter has a grasp
like that of granite, bracing,
and as a stone it seeks to still
all indices of motion.
This wind, though mobile, is no less hard,
and lashes out on water flesh
which huddles back and tries to miss
this solid synch with freezing.

A SPIRIT HEREABOUTS

It is like the grid of streets
and the thrust of buildings.
It takes its form from the patterns of bricks
and its being from the multiplicity of intent.
It is clean within its filth
and lonely among its throngs.
It is text and sound and rhythm
and weaves subtle threads of entrapment.
It is not only callous
not only light.
It works machines through the dark
and grows in places unintended.
It is all of these
and permeates the first breath of spring.

BY ORDER OF THE PRINCESS

"Hold down the thrashings
as punishments are detailed ..."
Red splatters, mixed with sweat and screams,
the writhing denials of pain
course through the muscles
as lightning shocks the nerves.
More retribution, more darkening,
more shredding of flesh,
all fill the time of no reprieve,
and teeth chip from gritting,
and hands bleed from clawing,
and the skin of arms lies open
from chafing against their bonds.
And the torturer smiles,
with teeth and leather gleaming
and whips dealing soul-crushing blows,
enforcing some repentance
and laughing all the while.

ODD ENCOUNTERS IN INAPPROPRIATE SETTINGS

They severally arrive,
each speaking the lines of different plays.
The amateurs tune up,
believing they have begun,
and the poseurs stand about,
seeking recognition of their mantle.
Fronts form
as though from ice cream melting backwards,
clotting from the mass:
each spectator sniffs the wind
to search the scent of their own fears.
Much gaiety sounds,
the titters of discomfort,
cloaked in shame,
as the swirl of the dance
is now commenced
and the scenes fall into synch.
Around strange orbits these actors move,
unknowingly eddy, and retrogress,
each dreamily following a well-pointed path
in sidled directions dictated by dread,
as bodies carried down to the deep
in the tornado downflow
of great ships seeking rest.

THE DANCING PITY OF THE WORM

It comes imbued with the stuff of ancestry
and refuses to turn to wine.
The stone is brushed and is blackness' mirror sheen,
the shrouds turn to handkerchiefs
and give solace to the mourning.
The hands of maidens turn monster in the grey light,
crossing the plateaus of being in the chariots of despair,
driven on by the rebellious chant
and steered by the eyeless sphere.
Corridors of endless entrance develop,
chaining doorways into the distance,
each requiring the specific words of passage.
    I do not know what need has brought me here,
    my words are of some other sound
    and my hands too clumsy to turn these ways.
    The diplomats of this stage move strangely.
    they confuse me by their bowings
    and the subtle shiftings of their feet.
    I have entered here without the script
    and can but dumbly stare at their expectations.
Air's addictions rush around this place
and a sickening light floods from the tomb;
the bones of these elders are immaculately bleached
and hold the gleaming scepters of their station
for eternity's slow inspection.

THE PURITIES OF GORE

Bleed, bleed, let blood,
cause blood to flow,
for this is the ritual.

    thus: Unto your enemies bring a knife,
                   their blood is power,
                   spilt for sun and rain.

    thus: Unto the Deity perform self-rending,
                   your act is power,
                   expressing true devotion.

    thus: Unto your self enforce reflection,
                   the sacrament is power,
                   bleeding from the mysteries.

Life ebbs and palpitations fade
as the self's twilight spreads onward
to a calm tinged of crimson.

Bleed, bleed, let blood,
come to purification,
for this is the doctrine.

        Shed blood as seed to bloom a spirit,
        to tap the rivulets of forceful life,
        to grasp the power of these passings
        caked and putrid with the wash of gore.

UPON THE LUNAR THRONE

Almost a madonna
given in these eyes,
bursts of pure expression
and controlled acts of sight
lash out from throne-room windows
to sanctify the realm.

Here make the supplications
unto the seat of need,
the ever-pulling vortex,
the dark receptive void,
the pleadings come heeded
in the toll of bells
and the tinkling voice of chimes.

Well ruled, this land,
under blankets of her thrall;
it is a happy people
who wear the symbols of her power
against the cold and awesome night.

SUICIDE PARABLE

He was lost and knew not where he was
He wandered blindly in the lands of amphetamine delusion
And he became lonely and mad
And he heard the voices and sounds of vengeful beings
And he wanted to love
And he wanted to be loved
And he hatefully fell in love once more
Dreading his action but savoring the imminence of pain
For he hated himself in all his weakness
And he loathed his wormlike mortality
And he was drenched in the need to swallow other souls
That they give him solace in his limitation
So nighttime fell and his solitude copulated without end
And spit out the bitter children of his hate
Who turned upon their father and reviled him
And tore into his flesh and into his soul
All screaming "Die, you who know you are the lowest!"
And he desired to die because none could see his world
And in his world there were naught but him
And he was all the void and totality of his world
And in his void he shed the acidic blood of his anguish
And he bled a vast sea of repugnant ills
And soon it came that he sought a drowning
That he be killed of himself whose love could never return
Whose rage and hatred were always of the self
That he eradicate himself and his world
And leave behind all those to whom he'd give his love
But from whom he could never accept love
Knowing that he was forever cursed
Entrapped in the stone walled vision of a poisoned world

THE SAILS OF DEATH

They load the bodies
on board these ships
in the sweltering heat
of the midmorning sun
and ferry them off
to plantations of life
in the rumored lands
of the elders.
So soon is my turn
to ride with the dead
across the black waters
of the unbreathing sea.
The pilotless craft
steers unerring lines
and from the horizon
appears with new seed
that our lands may flourish
and our children grow fat.
Few days are left
of the blistering heat
that calls up the boats
that journey to night
soon they will call
the names of new dead
and I shall be seeing
the golden temples
on the other shore.

THE VISIONARY'S CREED

I have seen the city darken
and have watched the woodlands die;
I have smelled the smoke of chaos
and seen fire rain from the sky.

I have run through nights of bloodshed
and done battle with the beast;
I have been to Satan's hallways
and rejected there his feast.

I have called forgotten powers
and have asked of them their aid;
I have sought the shrine of being
and unto its masters prayed.

I have traced the lines of ending
and spilled out the sands of time;
I have spoke the words forbidden
and been murdered for my crime.

I have braved the outer madness
and have stayed free of its trance;
I have turned the veil of matter
and joined briefly in its dance.

I have shattered with the cosmos
and so glimpsed the realms of light;
I have borne the curse of vision
and received the chains of sight.

SINISTER SUMMER DAYS

The dog's bone rattles
in the soft haze of a besotted afternoon,
strange bells toll wearily
in the indistinct distance
as though to mark a funeral march
or some wedding feast gone slow.
No birds sing in this heavy air,
no sounds of upper chambers
echo for the village;
unhumid dust swirls
and plasters itself to the skins
of all sweating wood and glass.
Occasional breeze is heard
in swinging signs and creaking frames
while subtle sounds.
like blankets dragged cross carpets,
stalk the woods
searching out the desperate scurries
of the warm and succulent
children of the forest.

ARID, FOUL

dry duck
dry duck
drugged drums drumming
druid duchess drowning
dry duck

      dolmen, dolmen
      who's in the dolmen
      five men, six men
      three kings and a pipe

dry duck
dry duck
drone drivel driving
dread dungeon draining
dry duck

      doppelganger doubles
      evenings full of trouble
      its mirror is off
      and needs a good wipe

dry duck
dry duck
dry duck
arid fowl today

THE SCHEDULE OF DEATH

This, the time to die,
to book passage
on long boats to the dark land ...
I try to turn the chalice
and without abdication
refuse the prophesies,
but all is naught
as these bowers close around
and my life is ebbed
away from me.
Can any hold these days forever
and know clear dawns
of eternal spring?
Can a summer's evening
be so elongated
that never once its magic slip?
No, these moments
are fast receding
that mark the numbers of these last breaths.
How is a peace to be so cradled
that transfer come in perfect rest?

SEEING IN

Caught looking at the spires
of the village of left overhood
tears streaming down cheeks
of soft metallic dew.
The visionary dance
is all that we recall
and we have lost our last chance
to scale those gleaming heights.

So now you know the sorrows
of the tale of the race;
add tears for company,
weep gladly at your fate.

Five are the towers within its walls,
all are similar but for their names;
their nimbuses glow with attribute
and pulse in function of their stage.

I try to speak but am rendered mute.
How can the last words sing
when lead has filled the sky,
how are its winged denizens
to know at last the truth?
I try to run but am handed death.

THESE THINGS UNDONE

I shall be as the ancient sages
and compose a poem upon the advent of my death.
Every day will I write this poem,
in all my acts the letters will be written out,
and I shall laugh with the symmetries
and sing soft sorrow at the rhyme.

I will take the air
and snatch from it petals,
pink, gentle,
clad in smoothness born of silk;
and I shall build of them
a vast and holy palace,
a blossom-fortress beaming light.

I shall walk the paths of conflict,
my face a warrior, set to its way.
I shall shake the clouds for thunder
and rock the stone foundations of the earth
that all may know my coming,
and know the wheel has run its course.

HOWLING BEHIND THE SKY

The moon sets traps
to snare the stars,
its webs of anger
drape the heavens,
a sickly green envy,
a hatred of sunhood.

Dark currents pull
within constellation bounds,
they turn and twist
and pull the wisps of untrained matter
into their silent sway,
the night forever is their lair
and waiting is their curse of life.

IN THIS DARK PLACE

Facets shatter
and pools of habitation
are barely stirred
by plunging fragments.

This is a sea of stagnation,
a thick broth of ill decay,
its form is stillness
and holds viscosity so deep
that action lives doomed
to stillborn birth.

And, hopeless dwellers
seek to swim
and seek to make constructions
and order in the mire;
their spanning crystals rise,
triumphant beams of concept,
only to be engulfed
shard by shard again.

ALL OTHER GRAVE DECISIONS

Swirling, swirling,
mists across the field,
cold as winter,
denser than the pyre.
What shadowed figure
lies pregnant in this veil?

Night is rife with doors,
All opened by the key of thought,
so still the whirling mind
lest too many entrances be granted
and too many spectres brought.

The game of difference
has but one name,
its hosts will riddle
and its language change,
but in its calling
the many are one
and in its service
dissolves all multiplicity.

EMPOWERMENT

Into the land
of silent children journey,
within the woods
of apprehension stay,
among the crowds
of massed unthinking tarry,
unto the gods
of isolation pray.

It is the dark
that holds the spirit captive,
these are the walls
that hands may never break,
yours is the soul
that stirs forever pensive,
such is the road
that you alone must take.

Reach for the guides
of hidden vision's seeing,
call out the names
of spirits pledged to aid,
unsheath the sword
of warrior wisdom's being,
relive the lore
of other journeys made.

SECRETED, SAFE, AWAY

Small,
small enough to hide
and I know of concepts
floating in the void.
You, you speak of reasons
and things grasped by your eye;
I am all ignorance
and blinded by eyes
with amputated hands.
No, the items of this world
run round and through me,
I can not stop them to take account
but only slow them,
making unsubtle brushes
against their flesh.
Tiny corners,
yes,
these are the good places,
nooks of all the secrets,
where scriptures have been hidden
and angels dance and sometimes sing.

AS LIGHT THROUGH HAZE

so these things are taken up
of the space between stars
so these things are built upon
the shallow confines of reality

they are as visions
insubstantial
they are as thoughts
passing
they are as mists of the night
pregnant with the spirits
of those beings long lost
to the material plane

the garb of venue
this holds
it defines the cloaking order,
the path of obscurity
this delineates,
it marks the milestones of arcana

free, free
the enslaved mind
from all these shackles
loose, loose
the rampant seer
upon these planes

HEARING FAINT THAT FINAL CALL

It is probably good,
the not owning of weapons,
for far too often
the suicide call wells up
and feels the sole path
from these constrictions.

Were there but some other door,
some less confining hallway
leading on to better lands;
but all in this life is crushing,
the weights of loneliness
that press against the weights
of useless employ.

All hope is for escape
but this world winds tighter,
pressing out all breath and joy
and leaving nothing
but desolation
and the beaten soul.

IN HER NO RAGE

Hands press to temples,
cooling as ice,
calming as the end of wind.
Sacred sister,
how you douse the fires
of insane rage
and pull from sneers
a soothing smile;
into your depths
all shattering tumbles,
before your calm
all anger takes flight.
What arcane gem
cedes you this power,
what holy spell
is wielded by your mind?
Please place your hands
on me again,
please touch me softly
with your night.

IN YUCATAN

many dead things
are found at dawn
in Yucatan
no road is safe
to cross at night
this place too old
to learn the ways
of driving steel
of modern man
these snakes and dogs
and forest beasts
all lie in blood
their guts hang out
the flies descend
the sun bakes ooze
in sick'ning spills
too old a place
the Yucatan
its ways too set
to move with man

TEXTURES OF THE DAY

These days are rank
with the smell of entrapment,
their battlements waft
thick through the air.

These days are deep
as the pit of damnation,
their fabric pulled down
by some word or deed.

These days are soft
and the essence of cotton,
they suffocate time
and muffle the where.

These days are held
in the grasp of the rain god,
they center the mind
and cradle the seed.

These days are high
as the clouds of the morning,
crystal and shining,
flying on light.

These days are old
with the lore of these buildings,
they scream out of time
and echo their age.

These days are spun
in the workshops of movement,
they harry the earth
and pester the night.

These days are iced
and caught up in clearness,
culled from the stars
they drop on this stage.

A RUDDY COURSE AND LINE

Is the curve faulty
by lip or by glass,
are ragged edges
the plea that wrings from eyes
the heart-voiced flood of blood
washed rampant,
deluged of fields
all lands bearing and barren,
beholden to my name?
So it is and held open,
the sanctum profane is the tablet,
it is the broken vessel,
it is the signing line of fools.
There is no drying here,
too wet to walk
gore washes up, crusts the walls,
the streets of old amphibians
too long gone to hold their turf.
Knock and knock
the doorway is unblocked,
your eye is the lock
your mind the steel entrapment
of all your petty prisons.
Blade this dark,
black cutting edge,
it reaches sin through no defense
and splits open rivers,
slighter currents,   '
tsunami of the dying age.

WHY EXIT IS NEED

The worst part is
when you find out
that the universe is sinister
and hates you as deeply
as you know you could hate yourself.
It is at that instant
that all hope and joy become hollow
and all pleasantness becomes an empty farce
and you realize that nothing, nothing
is worthy of salvation in the common, human world.
And, when you start to look
for a way to get out,
for a way to be free of that hateful self
which is chained so tightly in that web of evil,
you find lies, pretty fantasies,
idiocies built up to please the subtler greeds
of that phenomenal pit and its denizens.
Nothing of this world
will let you out of this world
and all of this world
seeks to smother the tiny spark
which is not of this world.
It causes such hatred to flare up
that I would have the universe put out,
hoping in its ashes
to finally find a door.

REMOVAL FAR UPSET

Watching time sneak out
through spaceless seams
in worlds and beings
to other forms,
through tears she cried
"Are any stronger?"
and froze upon the pedestal,
a victim of the virtue, grief,
an emblem rising of morose rites.
All, all true,
no guile or falseness,
this land too thick to cede a lie,
its cloak hangs deep with nameless sorrow
and dull, and dull, once hopeful minds.
Not much of spans
give up to freedom ways of taking,
they more to circles run
and batter down the grasping hand;
no course has come
to guide the homeless
here set adrift,
in search of land.

FOR ONE UNAMED

Elemental lady
how smoothly unwraps me,
peels off the bastions
of brick and of fire;
a child of wide journeys
in strange years encountered,
both cradled and held
as day cedes to night.

So sweet the disruption
in hours of travail
as secret desires
hang tense in the air;
such smiles are to blossom
in intimate playings,
our dear hidden game
by others unseen.

Please break this aloneness,
destroy isolation,
bring beauty and joy
to shadowy life;
in you is the power
for lightening spirit,
thank you for bringing
relief to my day.

H.H.'S IMAGE

Rinpoche has given
an inestimable gift
for I am new
and weak of vision.
No more the complexity
of color and face
will stress and depress
with Kalachakra;
no more the myriads
of compassion bearing arms
will dismay my hopes
with Avalokiteśvara.
New visualization
has been detailed,
so simple and so lovely:
     Two arms, two legs,
     a single head,
     with vajra, bell,
     embodying the dharma,
     alive with grace ...
     how easy to see you,
     Tenzin Gyatso, Dalai Lama.

NEW COLD COMING

It is the season
of small birds' dying,
their broken bodies
lie near hard glass.
They litter pavements
with their colors,
their feathers bright
on still cement.

Not here, not now,
not of these canyons,
concrete and steel
and brick and slate,
this turning is
of other native,
of forest, glade,
and mountain born.

That clock again
has called to folding,
to loss, to dark,
it sounds retreat.
The cold invades
in tiny tendrils
that grasp the night
with subtle pain.

ILL VISION, DREADED SIGHT

The blue bands
of steel machines
hover in the grey,
softly singing metallic songs;
these oblongs seem to wait
some time, some coming,
the brutal hand of change.

A pop, a crack,
a breaking sound
dissonantly spikes the whine,
a red, red tear
rips metal skin,
a slow burst comes to ships
like pods too ready
to shed their seeds.

What wings have born
of shelled machine,
what crimson hide shines moist,
newly out from birthing place?
These necks, these eyes,
these flaming manes,
will none defy
these dragons' hate,
nor bear the crown as victor?

ONE NOON AROUND

Pigeons puffed,
sunning silent,
unhurried squirrels
search for food.
I, keyless, am here too
at Gramercy Park,
a nest of peace
in the chaotic town.

SNACK TIME

The other pickle
is driving me nuts
sitting in a jar
in the fridge
like some greenish whale
in a green, green sea.

My teeth reach
like Soviet harpoons,
my teeth tear
like Japanese ships
for processing flesh.

Too late to save,
this little whale
is ground to feed.

DISTANCE AS SEASON

The virtues of removal,
taken up in times of change,
these are the face and soul of multiplicity,
the errant seed of man and age.

No thing holds tight to now,
no name sticks well in course's flow.
I enter and return,
giving meaning to each day, each hour,
feeling and reactive
opening flowers bloomed that we know.

Loss and vision,
in words set all wrong
in frames unright and fields
not of the slighter rain
nor synaptic journeys
to other's placing pigment,
this is a trekking,
all alien to this land.

No, no, we know,
our knowledge goes beyond that bound,
no passing is untangled,
unentered in that log.
Our angels free these vestige chains,
they hold the torch of speechless seeing;
may they lead true on,
vanguard to our day.

CONTAINED WITHIN RESENTMENT

Sickness wraps its tendrils,
dripping hints of rage,
unsubtle wisps of anger,
round and round this form;
a twisting tears at resolve,
a ripping insists towards fury,
and yet resistance holds,
to destruction's end resistance holds.

Sound buffets,
sight brings stinging enticement,
touch is only pain,
taste is but chemical,
only chemical;
where is the world,
lord, where is the world?

No hold is granted
to grasping hands,
no hope is granted
to grasping minds,
scant holiness enters
this grasping soul.

RENEWAL COME AT LAST

Sweet return,
blossomed like an unexpected bloom,
come sudden in unintended night;
I savor the richness of that scent,
the lushness of that texture,
the beauty of that presence,
come almost as a gift.

Soft confusing mists
hang lazy in the opens of my mind,
unsettled intent hangs unfinished,
uncertain in the hazy apparition's
unhoped actuality.

Do stay, do say
bright clear sweet things to me,
envelop me as finest melodies
playing through the air;
turn open night as were it day,
fresh, new and sunny,
filled with spring.

CAN SHATTERED BE REPRIEVED

Chanting borne on scent,
the seminars of restless aging:
rains have come by request
but settle little,
so held by stone.

I am not of this,
even these,
I am apart, in limbo,
I do not even touch their worlds.
Broken, all is broken,
the last defining has been to trash;
I am not me, not any's one,
not free in void,
jailed in brutal empty cage
called all my own, my owned.

The words and days rush,
flying pointless, all dull and dead,
I am like a corpse,
my will is cold, my spirit grey.
Soulless transfer into stone:
        the hours are wasted
        donated to breath,
        the sun is a phantom
        its phasings have no point.

So, come with me, who would?
Would any freely take the grave,
a living grave of life unlived,
unfelt, unsavored, in choking bonds
of societal propriety?
A fool that'd be, a hopeless fool.
Would someone pray
to be released,
would someone wail in sorrow's mourning?

FOR DEBBIE, #2

How can this be?

What is this hatred,
this love?
What brings up acidic aching
for release, for dismissal,
for attainment or destruction?
I despise it,
I loathe its grasp.

Your name,
bitch,
your face
is all that I see in the sweaty claws
of nightmare time.
Your absence, your distance,
your endless refusals recited on and on in my mind,
these haunt, these stalk,
these take up all the darkened corners
and echo madness, rage and hatred,
which spill their corrosive force
on a grossly implicate race.

You are the billions,
the insane rampant tumble of rejection
which is the voice of contempt, which is the hand
of ultimate denial;
which is the cage about me now,
which is the genesis of anger.

How could you hug me in this night?

Are you the spirit of Iscariot.
impassioned in Gethsemane to delimit the boundaries
of waywardness in an unfeeling people?
How can the arms of one such as you
who is now the essence of my pain
encircle, enfold, encompass that which you have shattered,
shredded, masticated and expelled,
spit out on the trash heap of emotion and hope?

From my eyes flow dark liquids,
the trails of prayers forgotten and decayed.
Their putrescence holds the rot of all my love,
all my care, all the feeling for this race.
It drips upon the curdling ground
which screams from contact, recoiling in terror
from agonies unnamed.
No more shall I love, no more shall I care,
no more shall this soul be rent by its seeding race.
The fire has been eliminated,
the soul has been snuffed out,
the heart has been scattered to the winds;
I am dead, an ash and cold,
what use can any affection be?

SOME NOTES ON THESE POEMS

This collection is in many ways a follow-up to my "Arise, Misanthrope, Take Stand Against The Race" book which came out in mid-1981. The poems here pick up from where that collection ended, covering selections from the second half of 1981, 1982, 1983, 1984, and through June 1985 when everything fell apart, my drinking stopped, and my Muse was silenced for nearly a year.

The present volume is a long time in coming, due in large part to the greater output of material that I was generating in the years represented. I sometimes find it hard to separate myself sufficiently from the poems to be able to edit with a truly objective eye, and so the task kept being put farther off into the future. I had hoped that the mass of the "editing" for this book would have been done by those dozen or so people who receive "folio" collections of my poems at the end of most years, but no response ever returned to my requests for this effort.

I hope that I have succeeded in pulling together a collection that represents the best of these years. The poems are arranged in the order of their composition to give a sense of their times and that downward spiral of life which is always leading "Into The Dark".

- B.M.T.

www.ingramcontent.com/pod-product-compliance
Lightning Source LLC
Chambersburg PA
CBHW071741020426
42331CB00008B/2121